D1613769

For the animals,
for Suzanne
+
for Simone

Photography by James BaloG

Designers: MassimoAcanfoRa, B.MarTin PederseN

Editor: ChelSey JohnsOn

Production: Dana ShiMizU

PubliShed by GraphiS

PorTfoliOs

PoRtrAiTs

AfRiCaN PoRtFoliO

AfriCan WiLd

THe Kill

OffsPriNG

ReQUieM

ISBN 1—888001—80—1 Printed in Hong Kong by DNP.

ExPlainiNG Wour own aRt can be a thank-

less task. The sapest stance by far is

to hide wiThin a castle of muteneS s,

pretending, as many artists do, to have said everything that needs to be said in the images themselves, rendering words superfluous. In some cases the work is so purely about visual effect, there truly is nothing to say. More often than not, though, contemporary art does have a philosophical or theoretical underpinning, but revealing it can make the artist vulnerable on a far wider front than if the engagement is based only on aesthetics: the more we let down the drawbridge and invite the viewer inside the ramparts for a tour, the greater the chance that the images and the ideas will, like the characters in Italo Calvino's fable, find themselves in a castle of crossed destinies.

Perhaps it would be enough to say that this book shows my passage through the animal world, wild and not-so-wild, and let the matter end right there. But an overwhelming compulsion forces me to unspool those rattling drawbridge chains and not be satisfied until the massive oak timbers settle in place across the moat. It is a perilous act, for both loyal allies and invading hordes will now have access. I can only hope the risk is worth the reward.

We live in a world of appearances and illusions, where little is certain. Politics, commerce, and technology trick us into confusing the authentic and the simulated; our most deeply held beliefs are open to argument and refutation. To a substantial extent, this has always been the case—and the history of the human mind and religious belief is nothing if not a history of coming to terms with this ambiguity. I am particularly enamored of the strategy taken in the Eastern tradition: it simply accepts that we are wrapped in a veil of illusion, known to Buddhists as maya, and that the ultimate goal of the human spirit is to one day pass through that veil into clarity. Hindus even have a major deity, the elephant god Ganesh, to facilitate this passage. But today we struggle with questions of what is real or what to believe more than ever, walking on the quicksand of relativity and postmodernism, denying ourselves any possibility of ever penetrating the veil, and barely even letting ourselves make a value judgement between the beautiful and ugly, good and evil.

In his classic novella "The Bear," William Faulkner sees the ursine as a symbol of what he calls the immutable power of nature and biology. Simply put, Animal is an expression of my own passage through the veil of uncertainty into the serene world of animalia and its steadfast power. Animals are whole unto themselves, completely poised in an existence bequeathed by five billion years of evolutionary rhythm, their minds and spirits focused. To look into the eyes of many animals, particularly the big ones like bear and elephant, is to sense a degree of calm and certainty rarely felt in people. Animal behaviorist Jane Goodall says that chimpanzees and people "differ in degree but not in kind," which is usually taken to mean that their psyches are much like ours, just more primitive. I propose that on the spectrum of what might be called existential contentment, animals surpass humans.

This is not to say that animals live in quiet bliss. The everyday horror of the relationship between predator and prey demonstrates that nature is not paradise. I profoundly dislike the tendency of environmentalism, going back at least to Thoreau, to over-romanticize nature. Nor do I suggest that animals be transformed into totems of New Age worship or mysticism. But I do believe that in animals we can find beauty, charm, intelligence, grace, and personality. When we question our status as the superior species on this planet, and revise our way of thinking about animals, the immutability we sense in them may open up a passageway to our own best selves, and to a world in which uncertainty segues into harmony.

This book was born from a lifelong quest to understand the boundaries between humans and nature, to look at the

interface between one animal species, <u>Homo sapiens</u>, and all the others. To me, that boundary has long seemed one of the most essential, historically significant photographic topics of our era. As a small boy, I watched the New York megalopolis consume the forests around my home. I climbed over bulldozed piles of loam and trees, inhaled the resin of splintered birch and the heavy-sweet fragrance of earth mixed with hydraulic fluid, watched flames carry away the wooded world and replace it with housing developments. Out beyond the subdivisions, in the remaining woodland, I discovered the secret lives of the animals who still lived there: whitetail deer, pheasant and turkey and grouse, fox and rabbit, even the occasional black bear. I resolved to touch those lives, both then and in an indeterminate future. At the time, the only people around me who gave much thought to wild animals were hunters, and with that role model as my guide, I killed so I could caress a pheasant's kaleidoscopic feathers or touch the magical sleekness of a deer. The idea of engaging the animals through photography had barely occurred to me, but I vividly remember that my first photographs, made at the age of nine with a Brownie box camera and black-and-white film, were of rabbits and squirrels.

Some years later, as the war in Vietnam escalated, I could hardly help reflecting on my beliefs and behaviors. One day, after killing a running rabbit with an arrow through its heart—the kind of shot hunters like to extol as perfect—I watched its dying agony and realized it was inconsistent to tell my draft board I was a conscientious objector to the senseless killing of people in a faraway jungle, yet at the same time cause senseless death in my own forests. I stopped blood sport that day forever.

As I left hunting behind, I soon discovered other pleasures in the outdoors. Driven by the sheer love of wildness, I climbed hundreds of ice faces and rock walls from Alaska to the Alps to the Himalayas, to summits that in some

student in the science of mountain environments, I was deeply involved in studying the worst flash flood in the recorded history of the Rockies. Eventually, the camera became a vehicle for recording and engaging with all I saw as I pursued a career in documentary photography. Within the space of a few months I might find myself living with fur-clad Inuit in the high Arctic, probing Siberian mountains never photographed by a non-Soviet, and plunging down rapids in the Grand Canyon. Volcanoes erupted before my eyes. Avalanches tumbled past my feet.

Yet somehow, those early scenes from the harsh contact zone between humans and nature, the forest destruction and hunted animals, never left me. Rendering them on celluloid soon became my life's work. Looking back, I am astounded that even as a wide-eyed, eager young magazine photographer, awed by my clients' every proclamation, I somehow knew that on my own I simply had to go beyond the conceptual and formal limitations of magazine work. I developed one small portfolio that looked at nuclear weapons installations in the Great Plains, another that considered loggers in northern California, and still another on hunting (the "Requiem" chapter is based on the latter effort, but more on that will follow).

By now, I was moving ever further away from some of modern photography's bedrock assumptions. One is that nature photographers should approach their subject with an objective realism, one that perhaps borders on a kind of creative passiveness. Another mandates that Homo sapiens is irrelevant in nature photography. Most importantly, nature photography is supposed to focus on an idyllic Shangri-La existing somewhere out beyond the civilized world, for nature, in the Euro-American tradition, is everywhere people are not. These assumptions were (and still are) far too limiting. I knew that my creative advancement needed not only new visual strategies, but different ways of thinking about subject matter. This par-

but different ways of thinking about subject matter. This particularly applied to the sub-genre of animal photography, which most photographers treated in a formulaic manner.

For a time in the mid-1980s, I did various magazine assignments in the world's great national parks. But I was not content with the work: I was troubled by the realization that these parks were relatively pristine islands in a sea of human-altered habitat, and that I was helping magazines disseminate a pleasant fiction about an endless Garden of Eden. Somehow, it seemed, truer pictures would symbolize the ever-present tension between the natural and civilized. In the midst of pondering all this, I went to the San Diego Wild Animal Park to photograph a rare and extremely endangered rhinoceros species for a National Geographic book. As a magical sunset glowed on the textured hide of a rhino standing four feet away, a creative lightning bolt hit. It dawned on me that this animal, and all endangered animals like him, needed to be photographed in a novel context. This context would resemble that of a classical portrait, a fashion study, or the chic photography of luxury products. The animals would be framed against simplified backgrounds of canvas or paper. Strobe light would reveal form, color and texture more richly than natural light ever could. Such a strategy would place beauty at the nexus of the pictures, while alienation, the alienation of endangered species that no longer had safe, secure habitat on this planet, would be the images' psychological core.

It is no small irony that I chose the devices of consumer culture for photographing things wild and pure. With each passing year, we are barraged by ever more visual messages intended to make us lust for extraneous material goods, and nothing could be further from the spiritual awe I feel for nature. But like it or not, the consumer juggernaut speaks the dominant visual language of our era, so why not, I decided, use its tongue to speak on behalf of entities that are intrinsically valuable? Could

there really be just one way to tell about our love affair with nature? I thought not, for it seemed that the rigid modernism laid down by Ansel Adams and other well-known landscape photographers two generations ago had become a straitjacket to creative innovation. It was time to move beyond this inheritance. Appropriating the photographic codes of consumer passion in the service of nature became the untracked continent I explored.

After much experimentation, I found that stylized portraiture yielded an enormous dividend: it led me into the secret labyrinth of the animal mind, revealing that intangible yet unmistakable force called consciousness. Ranchers, pet owners, and other people living close to animals accept as a given that much goes on in the animal mind. As many authors before me have discussed, science chokes off this awareness when it refuses to acknowledge that which cannot be measured. Happily, art is not constrained by the need for quantification, so I am allowed to assert that stylized portraiture, which was originally a way to symbolize the endangerment of wildlife, evolved into a means for me to see the indomitable, Faulknerian psyche of animalia. I hope the echoes of Ganesh's trumpeting call to clarity can still be heard in the chapter titled "Portraits."

Overlapping most of the period when these portraits were produced, I invested a great deal of energy in a project I call "Techno Sapiens." It explored the convergence of the human animal and technology. Much as I believed in the socio-historical value of producing it, "Techno Sapiens" had a decidedly masochistic quality because it required spending long periods in places I simply didn't enjoy. By late 1998, I realized the project could never be finished, yet was complete enough to be put aside so I could move on to other topics. Not surprisingly, I looked for something straightforward involving time in the sunshine: "African Wild" and "African Portfolio" are the result.

I had worked in Africa before, but blasphemous as it might be for a nature photographer to admit, I had never found the place as captivating as Alaska, the Himalayas, the American

West, or a dozen other locations. My indifference clearly had something to do with my earlier frame of mind, because when I visited Africa again in 1998 it was utterly exhilarating and overwhelming. The intensity of sky and stars... the granite and baobab... the gentle smiles and melodic speech of the people... the spectacular animal life. Even after centuries of environmental abuse by natives and colonials alike, the pattern of hoofprints in the powdery soil is so dense it seems as if the continent's crust must groan and creak under the weight of all those mammalian lives. No concentration of wildlife anywhere can compare with it.

So through South Africa, Botswana, Zimbabwe, Kenya and Tanzania I traveled. At first I photographed with the usual array of telephoto lenses and high-tech cameras. These images are in the "African Wild" chapter. But I wanted to reach a less technologized form of image-making, and eventually arrived at the tool used in the "African Portfolio" pictures: a fifteen-dollar plastic camera. It had just one shutter speed and a plastic lens with approximately the same degree of optical purity as an old-fashioned Coke bottle. But its directness and spontaneity were enormously satisfying. I was working at the simplest technical level possible without discarding cameras entirely. There was no fumbling around with lenses, batteries, filters, film changes, or a dozen other distractions inherent to professional equipment. It was all about the pleasure of seeing and being in three-dimensional space.

The duality of birth and death is the underlying theme of "The Kill" and "Offspring," two short chapters that deal directly with the most essential facts of life on earth. It could hardly be otherwise, for the paradoxical union of opposite realms, life and death, is at the core of existence: the death of one entity feeds the birth and life of another. The ancient mythologies have long recognized this inescapable truth. Mediterranean cultures pictured it as a snake eating its tail. The Hindu god Shiva is both creator and destroyer. Yin and yang cup each other like lovers. In the Christian tradition, the death of Christ becomes a means of cycling the life of the spirit back to those on earth. These chapters are a vehicle for exploring the animal aspect of that great alternating wheel of existence.

The "Requiem" chapter encompasses the darker aspect of humanity's relationship with animals. "Requiem" comes from a period between 1981 and 1984 when I obsessively photographed various ways humans manipulated the land and ecology of the Rocky Mountain region. I eventually concentrated on recreational hunting, the motivations for which can be argued endlessly without reaching a conclusion. Do hunters kill for meat, as so many of them like to claim? Or is it for other ends, like trophies, camaraderie, a good day outdoors, connecting with nature, or fulfilling a primal impulse to hunt and kill? All these factors play a part, but procuring meat is the flimsiest of the explanations, since the cost per pound of big game is almost always astronomical. In "Requiem," I choose not to pass judgment, but instead to follow animals being transformed into totemic remnants of their former selves. Do their spirits survive that transformation? I hope the pictures testify that they do.

One final point: At some level, the explanations I have given in the preceding pages are irrelevant, for every artist knows that his or her best work is driven by forces beyond the ego. Art wells up from the unconscious, reflecting psychological states that may be indefinable until years after a picture is made. Still deeper is another process far more mysterious than the life of an individual: somewhere out in the darkness, beyond our collective beam of light, images flutter around waiting for the right time to reveal themselves; when we are ready for them, an unknown breeze springs up and blows them into sight.

James Balog. Boulder, Colorado. Spring, 1999

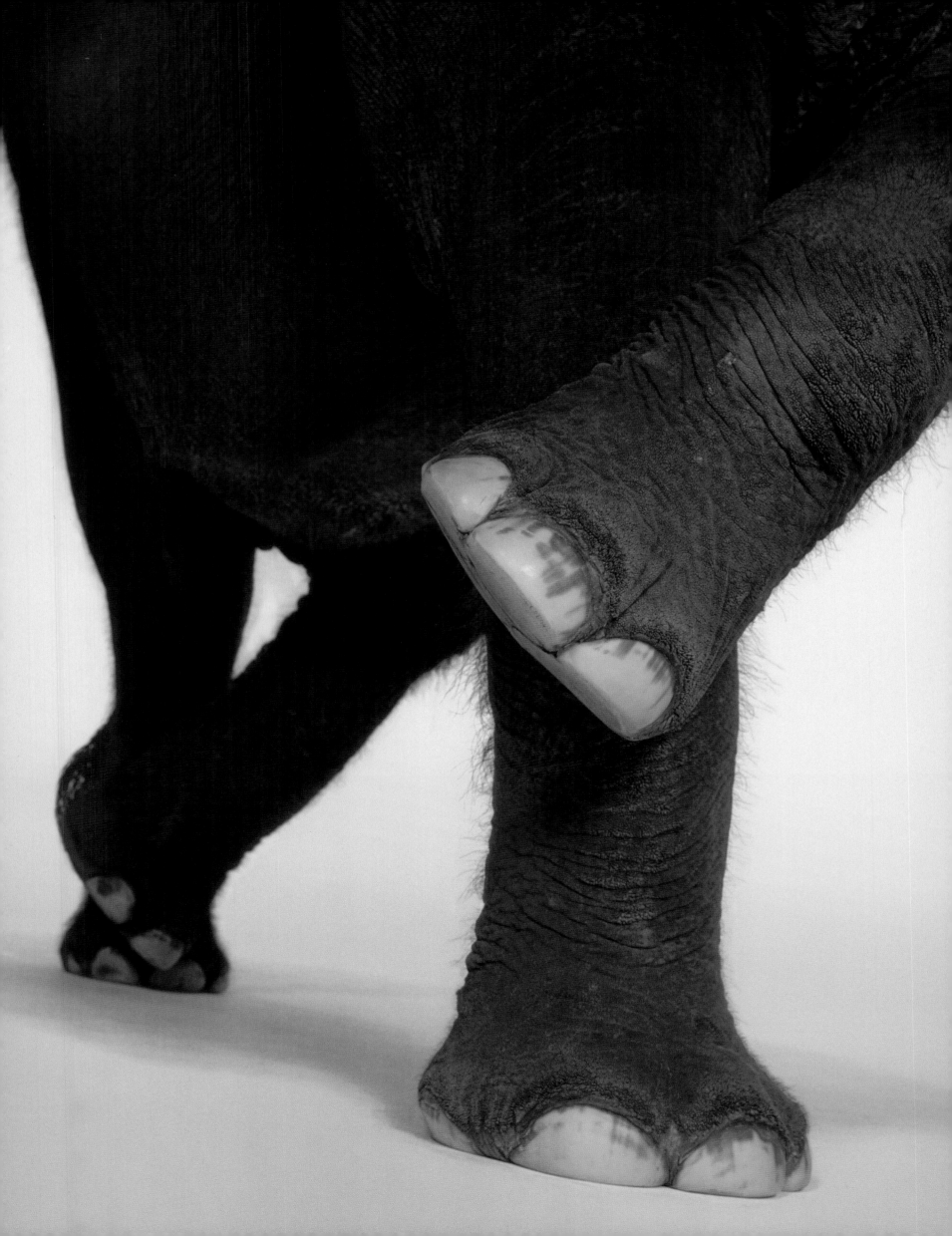

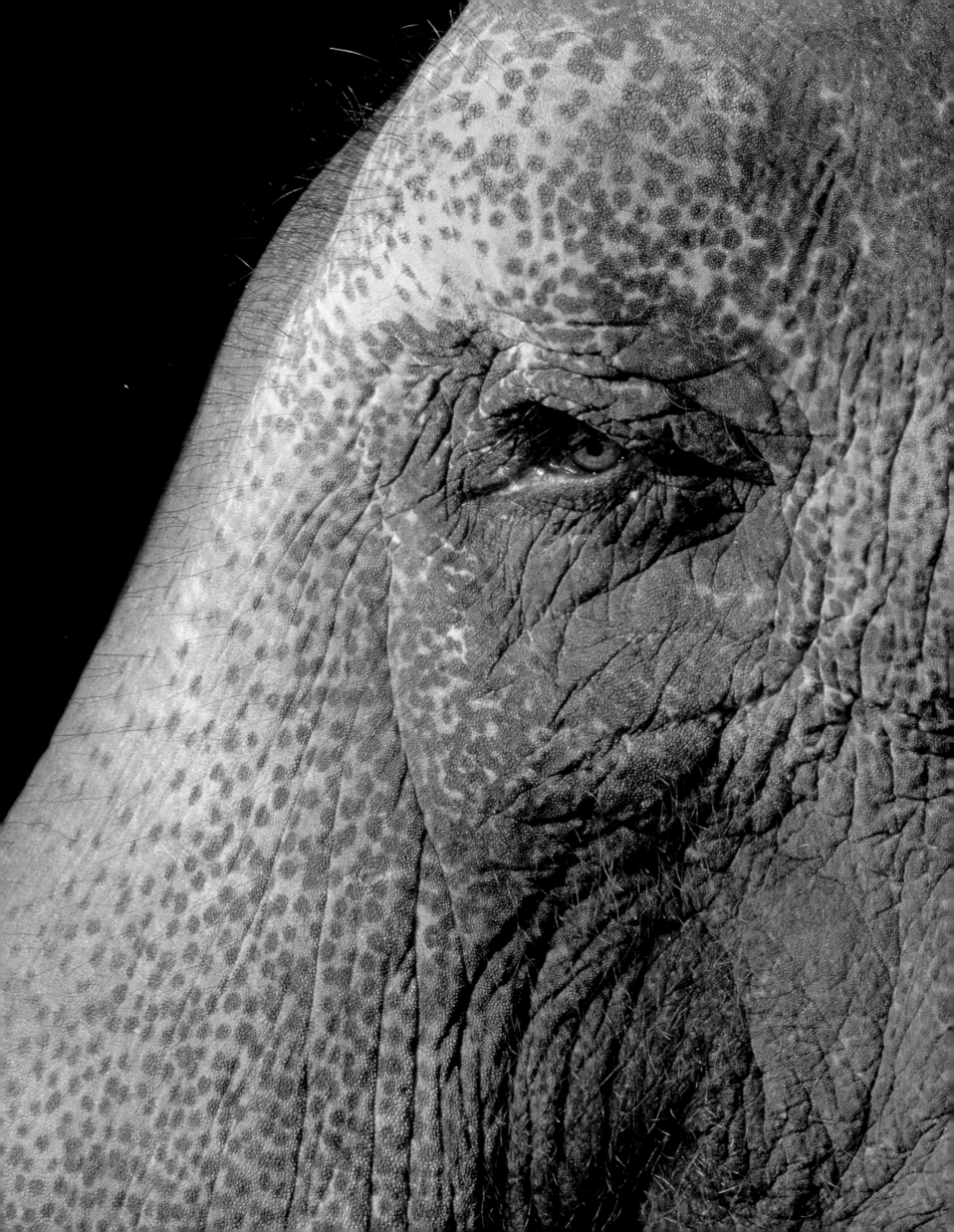

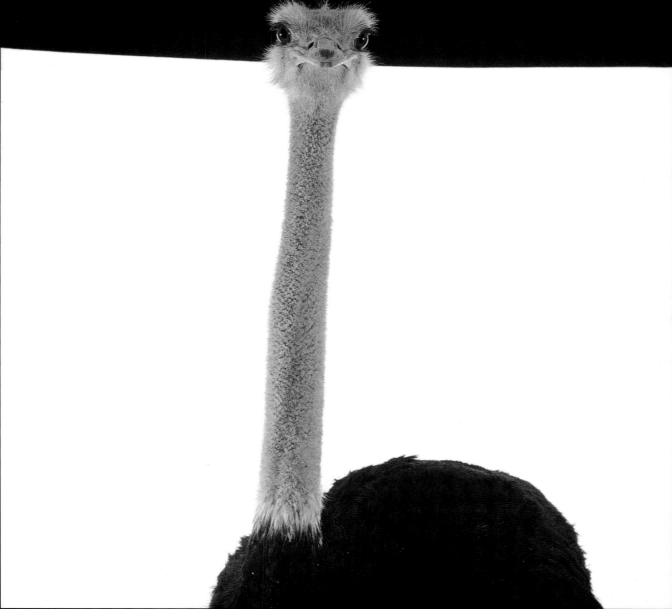

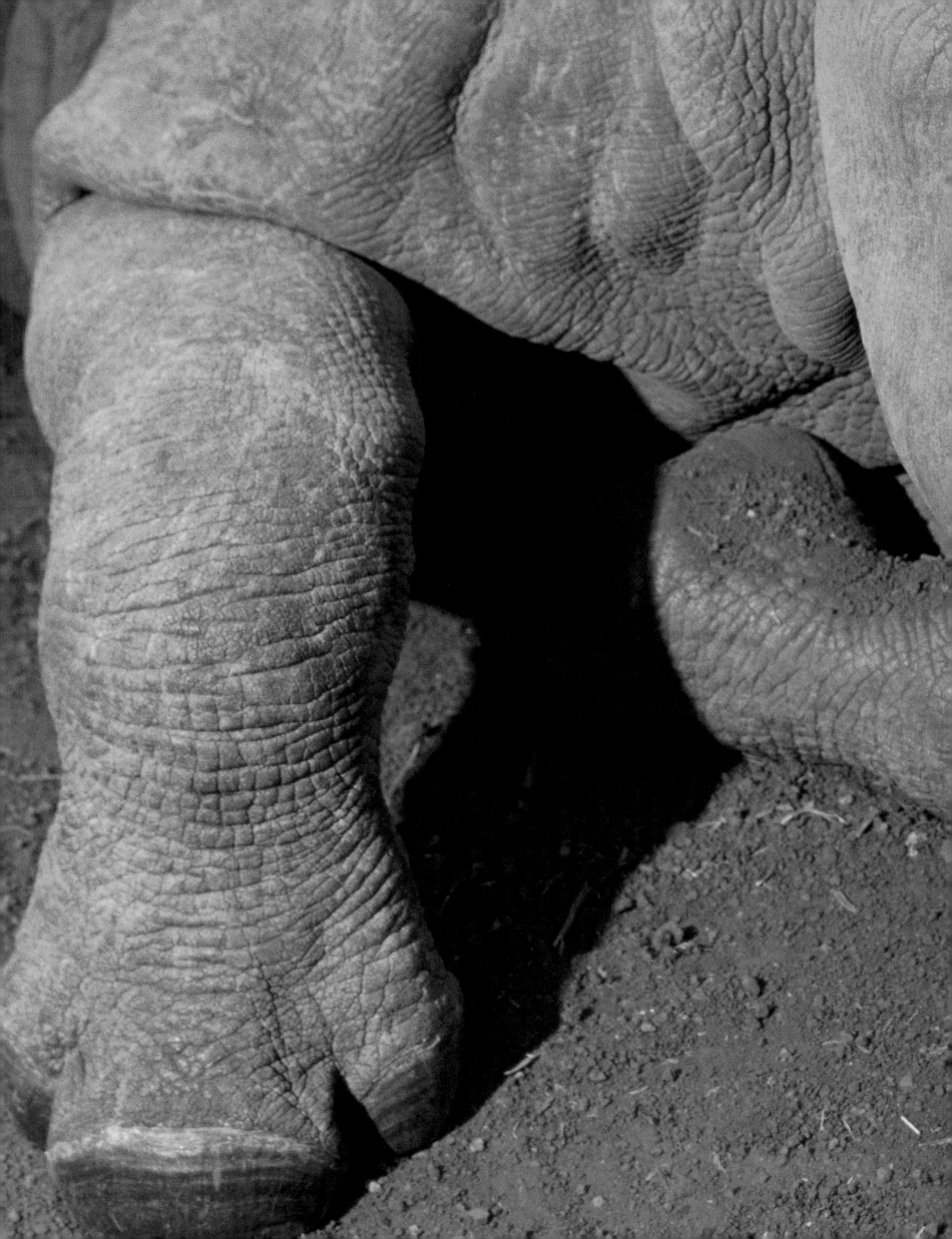

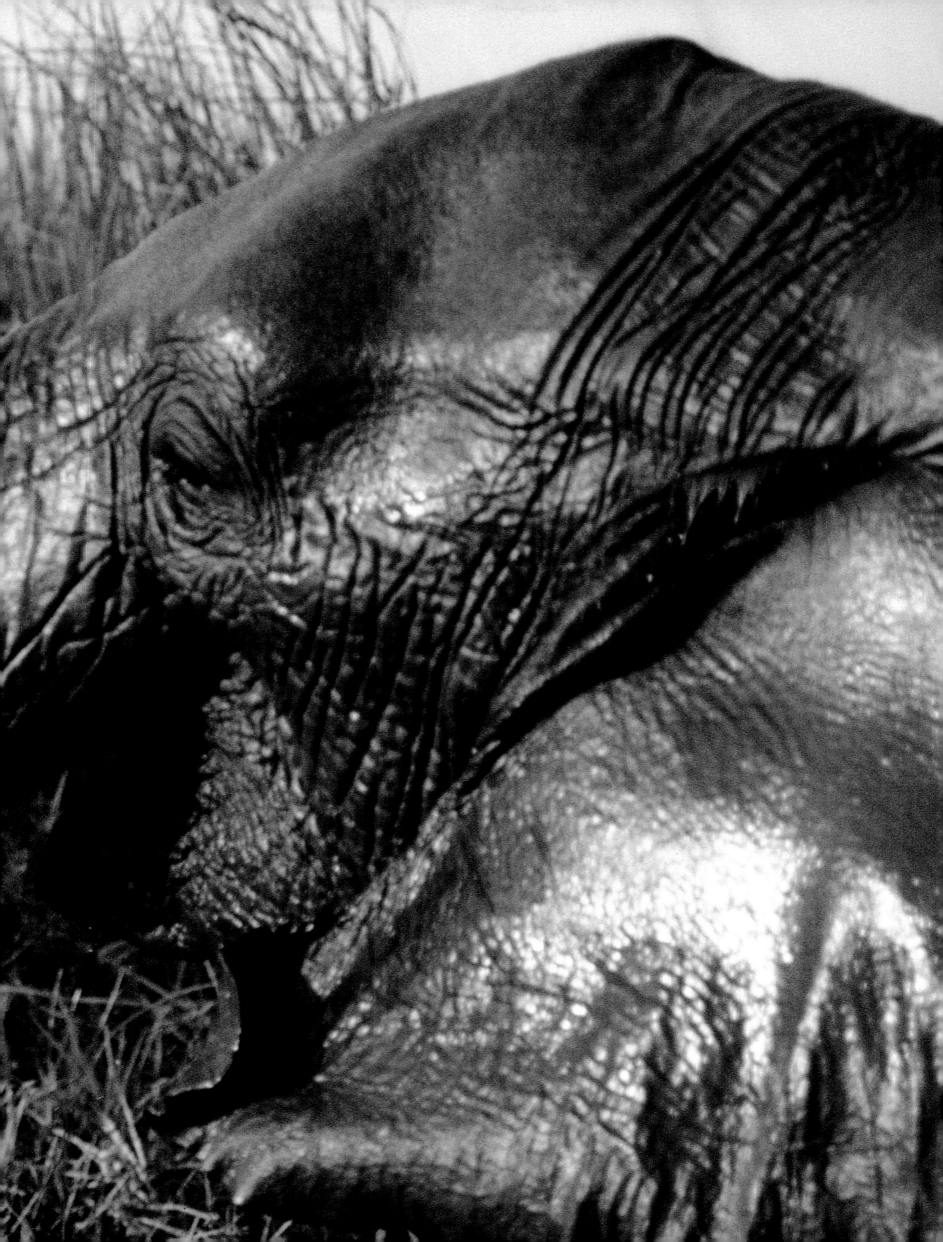

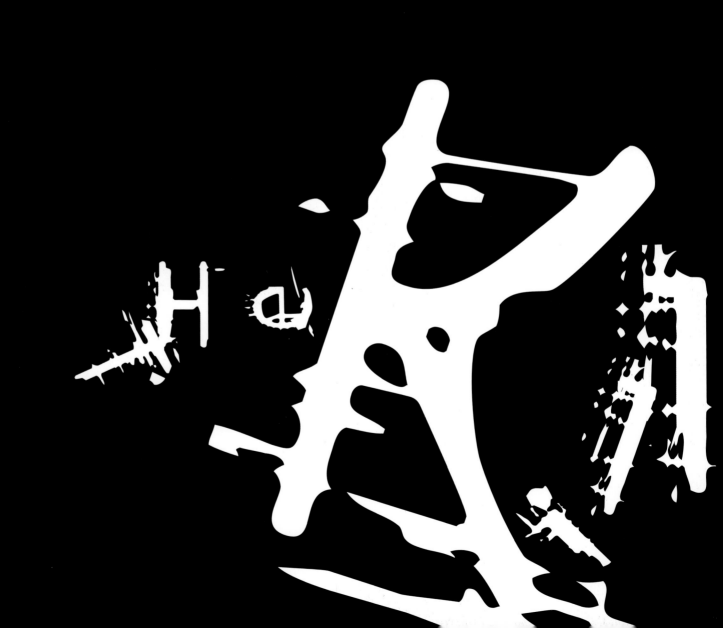

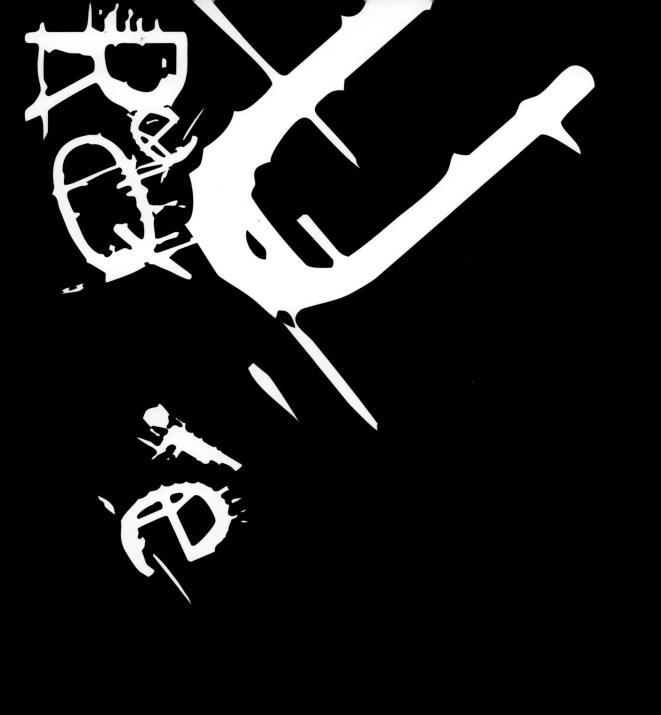

Photographer's Note:
It is customary in photography books to tell what
cameras and lenses were used. I have never really
understood why photographers are compelled
to talk so much about their tools, since they
are not nearly so important to the final outcome
as creative intention and craftsmanship.
I will say only that I used a wide array of cameras,
lenses, lights, and films appropriate
to circumstances and my stylistic goals.
A debate has raged in wildlife photography circles
about how pictures are made. Was a picture that
seems to document free-ranging animals actually
produced with captive, trained animals?
Was a picture that appeared to be the result
of great artistry and good luck in the wild actually
enhanced or assembled with digital technology?
Since these techniques are already well-entrenched
in photographic practice, I and many others feel
that they should somehow be identified when such
pictures are published. So for the record:
I trust it is obvious to even the most casual observer
that my stylized studio portraits were made
with captive animals. All the pictures that appear
to have been in the wild were indeed created
with truly wild animals, except for a very few
pictures at orphanages and research facilities,
all of which are duly noted in the captions.
Every photo with a white background was
originally shot as such. In the interest of rendering
them throughout this book with the same tint
of white, the printers decided to strip out virtually
all dot pattern from each background.
I used no other form of digital manipulation.

A Note on African Places:
I owe much to the people and animals at many
African locations. The reserves at Mala Mala and
Sabi Sabi in South Africa have some of the best
wildlife photography opportunities on the
continent, particularly for lion and leopard.
Depending on the season, Botswana has truly
amazing elephant photography: along the Chobe
River, I based myself at the Chobe Game Lodge to
be near the fords where the elephants swim to
Namibia; in Savute, at the Gametrackers camp;
and in the Tuli Game Block of southernmost
Botswana, at Mashatu Camp. Xakanaxa Camp
is a superb jumping-off point for a wide range of
adventures in the Okavango Delta. In Kenya,
Tortilis Camp lies at the foot of Mount
Kilimanjaro in Amboseli National Park and has
great access to the famous and highly approachable
elephant herds. Sekenani Camp, just outside the
border of the Masai Mara in southwest Kenya, is
well-postioned to work with animals and people alike.

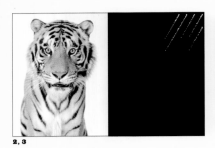
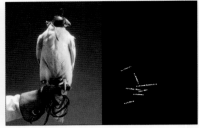

2, 3   4, 5   6, 7   10, 11

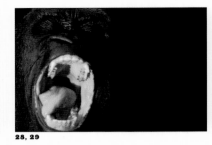
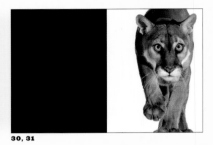

24, 25   26, 27   28, 29   30, 31

40, 41   42, 43   44, 45   46, 47

56, 57   58, 59   60, 61   62, 63

CAPTIONS

In this chapter, I prefer not to give detailed background information, but simply let the animal personalities speak for themselves. Each of these photography sessions was a great joy. No matter how late in the day, no matter how much traveling I had been doing nor how tired I was, these encounters gave me an exhilarating sense of breaking through that glass wall separating "us" from "them." Even in animals like reptiles, animals that our mammalian minds interpret as being mute and uninteresting, I came away with a distinct sense that I had met another psyche. The intensity of the pictures results from the confluence of two great rivers, the animal minds and the magic of the photographic process.

14, 15

18, 19

20, 21

22, 23

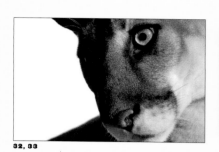

32, 33

34, 35

36, 37

38, 39

48, 49

50, 51

52, 53

54, 55

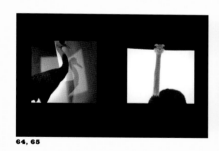

64, 65

66, 67

68, 69

70, 71

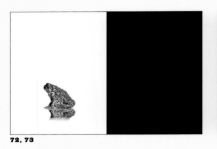
72, 73

74, 75

76, 77

78, 79

88, 89

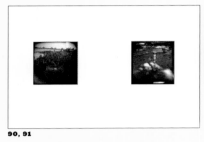
90, 91

92, 93

94, 95

104, 105

106, 107

108, 109

110, 111

AFRICAN PORTFOLIO

80, 81 Eighteen-month-old black rhinoceros orphaned when his mother was killed by poachers. At the David Sheldrick Wildlife Trust near Nairobi, Daphne Sheldrick and her staff are teaching him how to survive in the wild.

82 Burchell's zebra, Okavango Delta, Botswana.

83 Female African lion awakes from the activity that occupies most of her life. Okavango Delta, Botswana.

84 Waterbuck killed and partially eaten by cheetah. Kapama Game Reserve, South Africa.

85 Cheetah in the process of devouring a young wildebeest it has just captured in the Masai Mara National Reserve, Kenya.

86 African elephant bull on a 118-degree day in the Savute district of Chobe National Park, Botswana.

87 African elephant nursery herd of mothers and their offspring at the Chobe River in Botswana.

88 At this waterhole in the Savute district of Chobe National Park, Botswana, bull elephants milled around from mid-morning to sunset in search of the only fluid refreshment available for miles. Between two of my visits to the waterhole, there had apparently been a fight between some young bulls and this tusk was broken off. We turned it over to the park rangers.

89 African elephant bull in a state of mild sexual arousal gives himself a dust bath on a broiling morning along the Chobe River, Botswana.

90 Maraboo stork eggs on a tiny island in the middle of the Okavango Delta, Botswana.

91 The leg bone of a young giraffe caught in a snare.

AFRICAN WILD

94, 95 This is the same young orphan black

rhinoceros depicted in "African Portfolio."

96, 97 When European ranchers began arriving in Africa two centuries ago, they viewed wild dogs with the same measure of disdain that settlers of the American frontier did wolves and coyotes. The animals were vigorously hunted, trapped and poisoned, so that today they are essentially an endangered species in much of their range. At Mala Mala in South Africa, we had an unparalleled opportunity to photograph at close range the action at a den occupied by two mothers and ten pups.

98, 99 Millions of graceful impala prance across south and east Africa. Because they are a favorite meal for the big cats and are at their most vulnerable and unguarded while drinking, they are as nervous as race horses when at waterholes. Sooner or later, small groups duck their heads for a drink as others stand guard behind them. Kruger National Park, South Africa.

101 The matriarch of the "JA" family group in Amboseli National Park, Kenya. She allowed us to spend an hour with them at sunset. Elephant researchers have named her "Joyce," after famed biologist Joyce Poole.

102, 103 These adolescent male elephants just swam across the Chobe River and scrambled onto Sedudu Island [Botswana and Namibia have argued for decades over who controls the island, though Botswana is presently in control].

104 During the dry season of September and October, the Savute district of Chobe National Park, Botswana, is a desperate place for animals to live: excruciating temperatures, no water and shriveled vegetation make most animals flee to more luxuriant pastures. Female elephants and their young head north to the water of the Chobe River. The males stay behind, congregating by the dozens around the few points of water created where wells were drilled long ago.

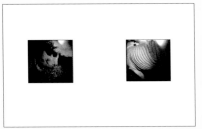

80, 81

82, 83

84, 85

86, 87

96, 97

98, 99

100, 101

102, 103

112, 113

114, 115

116, 117

118, 119

Since no females are available to stimulate aggression, the bulls are relatively benign and allow humans to approach them closely with a reasonable degree of safety. As a dust storm blows in, one bull greets another with a touch of the trunk, while the others take turns sipping the pure groundwater bubbling to the surface.

105 One day at Mala Mala in South Africa, we didn't vacate the path quickly enough for this female's liking. She made a most impressive charge at us, stopping only a few yards away.

106, 107 We were slowly motoring up the Chobe River in a small skiff when we rounded a corner and saw this sparring match between two teenage bulls. The tussle went on for ten minutes in the shallow water at river's edge. The animals were essentially oblivious to our presence, allowing us to approach within just a few of their body lengths. I was a bit concerned that a sudden misstep by the elephants could create a tsunami that would

swamp us, or even send them crashing into the boat. But with photos like this one happening I wasn't about to back away.

108, 109 During the annual dry season, the earth of the Savute district in Chobe National Park, Botswana, had turned to the consistency of talcum powder. A dust storm of Biblical proportions roared through late one afternoon. Finally, as the turbulence passed, the sunset appeared and this elephant trudged from the tired scrub.

THE KILL

113 A male African lion awakens from a day-long siesta, yawns, and leaves for a hunt at dusk.

114, 115 A male African lion has just killed a young kudu and is feeding on it. We made these shots during a remarkable five-day period at South Africa's Sabi Sabi and Mala Mala game reserves where we witnessed six kills by lion, cheetah and leopard at close range. After one of the lion

kills I wrote in my journal: "The most horrific scream that I, or anyone else in our vehicle, has ever heard shreds the night. It has a distinctly feminine quality to it, like that of a 12-year-old girl. We listen now not to the exquisite peace and harmony of night in Africa, but to the unbearable sobbing and wailing of a death which gives life to others. A catpaw slaps the antelope's head, holds it down for good and she expires in a last series of pillow-muffled cries. With eyes half closed, the lions tear at her with the kind of feral passion that humans can experience only during very, very good sex. From the beginning of the fatal encounter to those last sobs can be no more than four minutes, but the horror of it made it seem like days. For that antelope and every prey animal past and future, all of them sacrificed on the great altar of being, who knows how long it is?"

116, 117 A magazine assignment took me into a psychology research lab that was studying snakes [an odd topic for a psych lab perhaps?]. One of the

lab rooms was straight out of a horror film: open the door and fifty rattlesnakes buzz to life and coil into strike position. Though each snake was presumably ensconced in its own terrarium, I couldn't help wanting to flee such a nightmarish place. Behind the next door, we watched this brown tree snake settle into a dark dance with a mouse.

118, 119, 120, 121 Cheetah are the least powerful of the big African cats, but they compensate by sprinting at 70 mph, making them the world's fastest land animal. They frequently hunt in family coalitions, particularly coalitions of bachelor males [one such pair is cleaning each other up after a kill on the bottom right corner of 120]. Sometimes the hunt is a careful stalk; other times they simply wander along until they flush out prey, as did the cheetah with his jaws clamped around a duiker's neck. Their innate ferocity is in curious counterpoint to the little chirps and squeaks of cheetah vocalizations, a language that seems more appropriate to barnyard fowl than one of the world's great predators.

120, 121

122, 123

124, 125

126, 127

136, 137

138, 139

140, 141

142, 143

OFFSPRING

This chapter is the product of a LIFE magazine assignment about endangered species in captivity. All the species shown are under great pressure in the natural environment, primarily because of habitat loss and/or hunting. Zoos may be the last refuge for some species if natural conditions continue to decline, so those institutions are hard at work developing reliable ways of breeding and raising the animals in captivity. To meet our deadline, my assistants and I raced through a tour of seven cities during the Christmas and New Year's holidays in the winter of 1996-97. With such inherent charm, these young animals hardly need verbal embellishment, so I will just give a few basic facts on each.

125 Borneo orangutan, two weeks old. Hand-raised by keepers because she was rejected by her mother. Photographed at the Lincoln Park Zoo, Chicago.

126, 127 Greater one-horned rhinoceros, four-week-old female with mother. Native habitat: lowland forests of Nepal and northeastern India. Photographed at the Oklahoma City Zoological Park.

129, 130, 131 Cheetah sisters, ten weeks old. Native habitat: plains of Africa. Photographed at the Binder Park Zoo, Battle Creek, Michigan.

133 African penguin, six-week-old female. Native habitat: coastal South Africa. Threatened by oil spills and overfishing of its food source. Photographed at the Baltimore Zoo.

134, 135 Grevy's zebra, five-month-old male with herd. Native habitat: northern Kenya. Photographed at the Denver Zoo.

137 Chinese alligators, two years old [also seen on page 9]. Native habitat: Lower Yangtze River valley. Photographed at the Bronx Zoo.

REQUIEM

Some of these photographs were published in my first book, *Wildlife Requiem*.

140 The prairie is the scene of a continual contest between ranchers, who want to preserve all the fodder they can for their livestock, and wild animals, who of course are eager to feed wherever they can. Pronghorn antelope are a particular source of aggravation, so when hunting season began one October day, this animal quickly met its fate.

141 *Homo sapiens* has always been in savage competition with predators. In the American West, ranchers are especially hostile to coyotes, and pursue them with traps, poison and guns. After complicated negotiations, I spent one crystalline winter day in northern Utah with two decent and genial men, father and son, who had been hired to shoot coyotes from their helicopter. Working dawn to dusk, they killed seventeen animals.

142 Scene along the highway, Hell's Half Acre, Wyoming. One night in a private room at an Elks Club in Casper, Wyoming, the guide whose hunts I have been photographing is grilling me about my intentions. I have found that people are proud to have a camera see their kills for a day or two, but by the third day they begin to mentally envision what it is actually recording and become nervous. Now it is the night of day three and the guide is very suspicious of my affiliations. I am not sure I can escape this room without mayhem. At one point in the inquisition, after what must be the guide's ninth beer, he says by way of both defensiveness and alcohol-hazed aggressiveness: "It's too bad for the bunny huggers. When you come down to it, man is a hunting animal. Even though I can see the bunny huggers' view about not killing baby seals, man has by God fouled up the natural world and by God it's the duty of us to straighten it back out again."

143 A rural garage, Gardiner, Montana.

144 One Saturday morning, I opened a newspaper and learned that a scene of incredible carnage was taking place at that very moment in south-eastern Idaho. The locals, it seems, had so effectively exterminated the area's coyotes that they now had a tremendous increase in the jackrabbit population [normally kept in check by the coyotes]. The rabbits needed to be culled, so the plan was to place a line of people and vehicles

128, 129

130, 131

132, 133

134, 135

144, 145

146, 147

148, 149

160

across a huge field and drive whatever rabbits were hiding in the weeds into a small corral. There, they would be clubbed to death.

As fast as I could, I packed my cameras and caught the next plane to southeast Idaho. I arrived in Mud Lake at twilight to witness a nightmare tableau straight from Hieronymus Bosch. Teenage boys armed with baseball bats had waded into an ankle-deep morass of huddled, quaking rabbits and were frantically smashing their skulls. As night settled in and the glare of truck headlights illuminated the scene, the pile of skinned corpses quickly grew until it was chest high, twenty feet long and still mounting. Ten thousand rabbits eventually died. It was a family affair, so moms and dads, brothers and sisters, from the whole county were helping skin the animals. The little girl in this photograph wandered wide-eyed through the slaughter. Her picture felt like my own self-portrait.

145 The hunt that led up to the scene: We sit patiently on the flank of a small ravine, our eyes scanning back and forth, waiting for

the bear. Forty yards below us is a small garbage dump of bait that the hunting guide has been putting out for the past three weeks. The bait is composed of animal carcasses and kitchen scraps, but the real teaser are the marshmallow men swept up from the floor of a nearby Russell Stover candy factory. An hour passes, then another. Aspens thrash violently as a storm blows by to the north. For a moment, I can hardly believe that a being so wild as a bear will associate itself with such a silly exercise. The wind dies and a squirrel chatters.

A bear materializes. "Materializes" seems the only suitable word for this sudden, silent apparition of the beast incarnate, a bear. It paces calmly along as if on a quiet side street near home. Its fate is so simple: thirty, maybe forty seconds after it appears, a pencil-thick metal cone of no special significance smacks its front shoulder. The bullet catches the bear in mid-stride, its paw only inches away from the marshmallow men. It collapses, gives a little shudder, then moves no more.

It is a female. The hunter and guide peel off her hide, then stuff it in a backpack to become a trophy for the living room floor. Her meat, muscled and proportioned much like that of a human, lies where she fell, bait for the next bear.

By the time we return to the guide's home it is almost midnight. His wife is out of the house like a streak, and before he can say a word, she whines, "Honey, Pussy fell down the ditch and I can't get her out! I want my Pussy back." Much cooing and concern. The guide, bear blood still on his hands, dutifully trudges off into the sagebrush and soon emerges with a member of a favored species, known as a pet.

146 Macabre and bizarre though hunting scenes can appear to an urban, non-hunting population, hunters are usually proud of their actions. I met this man just as he was parking his car and preparing to hike up a mesa in search of mule deer. He invited me along on his hunt, which ended with this scene back at the highway four hours later.

147 Animal icons along the highway in a typical small

town in the American West. Dubois, Wyoming.

148 I made this image outside my motel room in Dubois, Wyoming. It makes me think of something the same guide said that boozy Elks Club night: "Hunters won't kill a doe because hunting's a man-on-man kind of thing. All these so-called meat hunters never kill a doe—and they wouldn't even if that was all they were allowed to kill. Imagine going home and saying you killed a girl deer?"

149 I devoted a good portion of 1981 through 1983 to witnessing humanity's conflict with grizzly bears and coyotes. Carnage and pain were the norm, but in the midst of it I found this tender moment between a young field biologist and a tranquilized coyote.

NEXT SPREAD
159 Argentine tree frog

LAST PAGE
160 Madagascar ground boa [also seen on page 49]

ACKNOWLEDGEMENTS

When a book is woven from the fabric of an entire life, singling out the particular people that helped weave it is nearly impossible. So much support and good will came from so many I barely know how to begin giving all the thanks that are due. In different ways, everyone mentioned below made an important contribution to creating the pictures in this book. I hope to be forgiven for just giving names. If anyone that I should have mentioned is left out, I hope to be similarly excused for a weakness of memory.

Robert Adams
Arts and Humanities Assembly of Boulder
Angela Baier
Jane Ballentine
Wolfgang Behnken
Howard Bernstein
John Botkin
Bobby Baker Burrows
Michael Brock
Bronica and Hillary Araujo
Cornell Capa
Howard and Jeannette Chapnick
Albert Chong
Rich Clarkson
Colorado Council for the Arts and Humanities
Robert Delpire
Ray DeMoulin
Ted and Mary Duffee
Grady Durham
Catherine Edelmann
Kathleen Ewing
David Fahey
Katarina and Thomas Farber
Larry Farrell and Dynalite
Charles-Henri Favrod
David Friend
Jane Fudge
Bill Garrett
Howard Gilman
The Goldman Foundation
Paul Gottlieb
Hal Gould
Bill Graves
Mark Grosset and Sylvie Languin
Sarah Hasted
Greg Hayes
Ray Hooper
Jane Jackson
Tim Jeffries
Vince Kamin
Margaret Kaplan
Tom Kennedy
Robert Klein
Kent Kobersteen
Robert Koch
Margot Klingsporn
Frans Lanting
Greg Lille
John Loengard
Mamiya America and Henry Froehlich
Robert Mann
Brian and Vikki McMillan
Andrea Modica
James Nachtwey
Grazia Neri
The New Lab and Tom Brock
Nikon and Ron Tanawaki
Joshua Mann Paillet
David Patryas
Cydney Payton
Photocraft Laboratories and Roy McCutcheon
Robert Pledge
Prince Bernhard of the Netherlands
Isabella Rossellini
Al Royce
Janet Russek
Kathy Ryan
Vinnie and Bob Sanz
David Scheinbaum
Marion Schut-Koelemij
Aaron Schindler
David Schonauer
Mel Scott
Dick Sheaff
Jeffrey Smith
Dieter Steiner
Michele Stephenson
Tony Stone Images and Stacie O'Connor
Nick Toth
Kerry Tremain
Anne Tucker
Diane Vanderlip

In addition, a few specific mentions are in order. B. Martin Pedersen is the leading light behind Graphis; he and Massimo Acanfora, the art director, are true geniuses in design and editing, and much of this book's character was created by their imaginations. Dana Shimizu and Chelsey Johnson were their superb collaborators.

Chuck Forsman, Jane Fudge, Bill Corey, and my wife Suzanne gave valuable help reviewing the manuscript for this book as it evolved.

John Wiltse, my primary camera assistant for six years, has given far more than his job description requires, becoming a great friend and ally. Other assistants who also made important contributions include John Lichtwardt, Frank Schaeffer, Zachary Epps and Kelly Corn. And I owe a huge debt to my studio manager, known only as Sport, who has been a smiling source of order, wisdom, and friendship for the past seven years.

My family has been an extraordinary source of support. My parents, James and Alvina, and my brothers, Stephen and Michael, gave so much in so many ways. My daughter Simone has walked with me down trails both bright and dark; she will be long into adulthood before she understands just how much she has meant to me and to my creative output. My wife Suzanne has brought peace and clarity to a life that has been turbulent for too long; her calm is actually the nourishment that allowed this book to be conceived. With typical good cheer she even tolerated long, hot days of photography during our honeymoon in Botswana and Kenya. Finally, my deep gratitude goes to all the anonymous animals who tolerated me and my bizarre photographic process. I wish there were some way to know how the results look and feel to them.

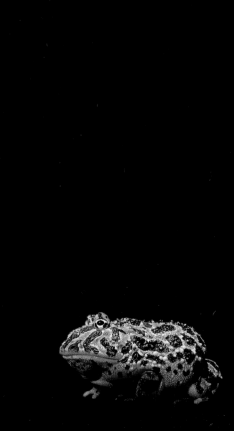